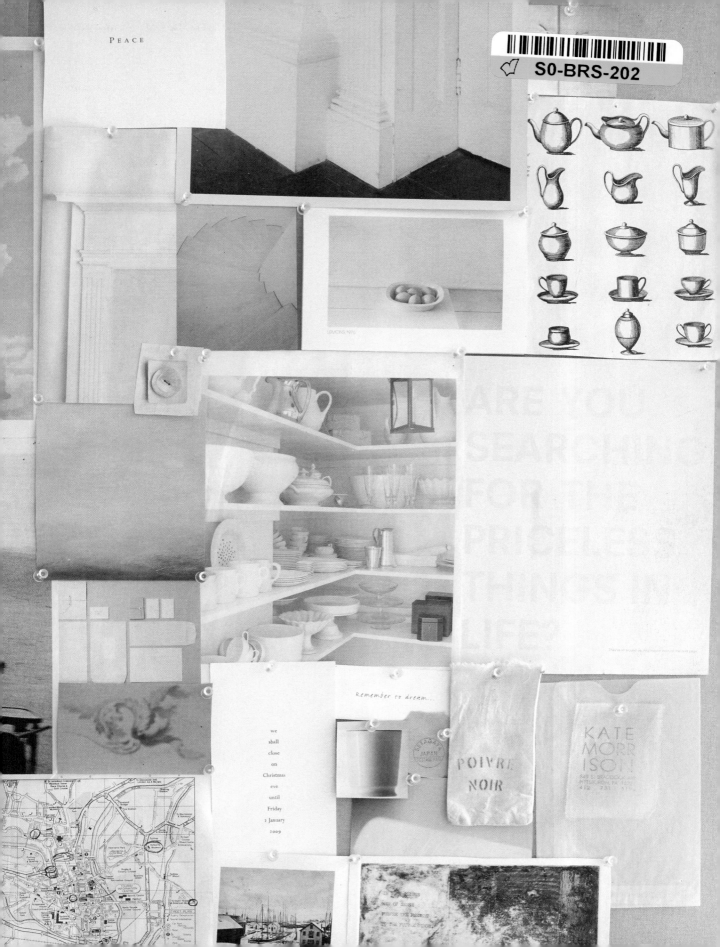

PEACE

Remember to dream...

we
shall
close
on
Christmas
eve
until
Friday
2 January
2009

POIVRE
NOIR

KATE
MORR
ISON

ARE YOU
SEARCHING
FOR THE
PRICELESS
THINGS IN
LIFE?

Life|Style

Life|Style

Tricia Foley

FOREWORD BY ISABELLA ROSSELLINI

RIZZOLI
NEW YORK

New York · Paris · London · Milan

To my family, who makes my house a home

FOREWORD

Let's play. Let me free-associate words that come to my mind with the name "Tricia Foley."

White, orderly, clean, calm, comforting, serene, simple, inclusive, warm.

You see, when I think of Trish, my mind automatically wants to linger in her home—around the details of her impeccable taste.

Having good taste may not be so important in the bigger scale of things, but Trish's taste evokes in me a set of emotions I like to feel.

When I visit her home, as soon as I pass through the front doorway I am enveloped in feelings of restfulness, serenity, and warmth. In fact, these feelings take hold of me even in her driveway. All is spare, organized, and clean. I instantly relax.

White is the color that dominates the interior, and Trish uses it to encourage the feeling of potential an artist might experience as he or she stands before a blank canvas: it is an invitation to creativity.

In this simple, white setting even a single flower, like a yellow daffodil in a transparent vase, can clearly spell out: "It is spring!"

Trish has found a way to communicate her observations, emotions, and thoughts in whispers, in a kind of restrained visual language. I find this language of simplicity very poetic.

Nothing in her home is cluttered, opulent, or intimidating. It is there that my brain, not having to react to aggressive stimuli, finds the perfect space to do what it is meant to do: think.

Inevitably, after a visit to Trish's house, I come back to my own with the intention to change everything and create a similar nest for myself. I ponder the idea of throwing away all that is not necessary, of simplifying, editing to the essential, organizing, and painting everything white! Of course, it may not be that simple, but Trish's sense of decor empowers me, filling me with great hope and optimism. It is contagious.

In fact, her determination to make anything old and decrepit beautiful is so contagious that ever since she moved to Yaphank, Long Island, the entire village has been transformed. Everyone seems to have renewed energy, wanting to take better care of their houses, streets, and paths that lead along the beautiful Carmans River.

Trish is always generous, ready to help anyone with suggestions and encouragement. She has restored several old houses otherwise destined to be demolished, helping to create the most charming and precious historical district.

When I visit other houses that are beautiful and tastefully decorated, I may feel dazzled and amazed. But often I am also left with doubts: do I have what it takes to have a beautiful home of my own; do I have the money, the verve, the ingenuity?

Trish's taste never makes me feel that way. Her taste is approachable. Her simple touches make it clear that money is not the essential ingredient—a single branch can be as beautiful as the most expensive arrangement of exotic flowers, a bucket as beautiful as an opulent vase. Empty wine bottles without their labels can become the most wonderful containers for cold teas and juices.

Her style shouts joyfully: "Everyone can have a beautiful home!"

— Isabella Rossellini

AN EDITED LIFE

I have always loved old houses and feel a strong connection to the past when I am in them.

I wonder who lived there, who loved there. I wonder what their furniture was like, what they ate for dinner, what they were reading, what their children's names were. What it was like on those icy winter nights when there was no thermostat to turn up. What it was like on those steamy summer nights when the fireflies were out and breezes blew in from the lake. When I hang my laundry in the sun, I wonder how many women did this before me, in this very spot. When I pick mint from the herb garden out the back door, I wonder who planted it a century ago—and I'm glad they did.

While growing up on Long Island, about an hour from New York City, one of my favorite rituals was when my father took the family for car rides to look at houses on Sunday afternoons. When I was thirteen, we moved into an unusual 1930s International Style house—I know I've absorbed some of its design aesthetic along the way. I remember walking inside it for the first time. It was so different from my grandmother's English cottage–style home.

Later on, I attended The Academy, a girls' school that was housed in a

A study in naturals—my friend Anita Calero, a photographer, asked me to give her ten of my favorite things, everyday objects, with which she created a beautiful signature still life.

nineteenth-century villa with high ceilings and wide marble stairs with wrought-iron railings. Art classes were held in an attic studio with large leaded-glass windows and skylights: I imagined that I was in a Paris atelier. During my college years in upstate New York, I would walk by old Victorian houses on the way to the ivy-covered building where my art classes were held and study the design of the shutters, windows, and paneled doors. My photography and art history classes were held in a new state-of-the-art concrete complex, which I admired, designed by I. M. Pei—but I would also leave campus to sit in the old village library at a big wooden table to read the latest home magazines.

I seem to keep falling in love with old houses, but I don't want to live too much in the past, nor do I think this appreciation for old houses and objects is a contradiction to having a modern sensibility in architecture and design. We all have our own style, a map drawn from family history, geographic influences, visual experiences, and personal interests. I am passionate about good design, whether it is contemporary or from the eighteenth century. Old houses have been time tested and seem to have a symmetry and functionality that I respond to. I prefer to open the windows for fresh air than turn on an air conditioner, and on cool evenings, I would rather put on a sweater and light the fire than turn up the thermostat. This appeals to the senses too, as the smell of the wood fire or a fresh bunch of herbs from the garden makes a home feel lived in. A basket of tomatoes from a friend's garden is more enjoyable to me than a fancy flower arrangement. And I like "editing" the things that surround me: collections, furnishings, words, clothes, colors, gardens. I want what's around me to mean something, and I don't want my life to be cluttered with useless or impersonal things. Everything in my home has to work hard to earn its keep. I love multifunctional objects. It's all a backdrop for my life, and I don't want to spend a lot of my time maintaining it. I've found over the years what works for me and how to streamline things, whether it is organizing closets, the kitchen, my office, or entertaining plans. And I am a firm believer in Henry David Thoreau's message to "simplify, simplify."

That doesn't mean I'm not a collector. I have too much china, too many linens, and far too many books. So the only way I can keep harmony in my surroundings is through editing. I take pleasure in arranging things. I can't help myself. I love setting the table, reorganizing the cupboards, folding a throw a certain way.

I'm sure that's also because I am used to arranging things for the camera and know how the results will look on a page. This is how I approach designing the rooms of any house, but especially my own—making my home a reflection of my life and style.

FALLING IN LOVE WITH A HOUSE

My first house—a white,
wood-shingled Long Island
half-house with a picket
fence—inspired a years-long
project of finding the right
materials, color palette, and
furnishings that would bring this
historical but woebegone
cottage built in 1845 into the
present. It was a labor of love,
respecting the architecture and
elements of the past and
creating a light-filled,
comfortable home for today.

I didn't expect to stay so long in this little orphaned house I found on Long Island years ago. It needed a lot of TLC. The shutters were gone, the grass needed mowing, trim was hanging off what was left of the porch. But all I could see was the proportion of the windows, the wall that hinted of a fireplace behind it, the wooden floors under the vinyl tiles. The frame was early nineteenth century, the chimney looked old, and the stairway was narrow, but everything had all been covered over in an effort to make it new. I wanted to take out the hollow-core doors and find old paneled ones to replace them; I wanted to fill the interior—all dark, cheap paneling with bad wallpapers and shag carpet—with light.

It was my first house. I had worked on many decorating and renovating projects for magazines, and rental makeovers on a budget were a specialty of mine, but this would be my own house done in my own style. It was a design lab for many projects to come over the years. It was soon filled with shades of white, in the form of freshly painted walls and open shelves with collections of white pottery and cupboards stacked with linens. Yard-sale finds were mixed in with an antique crystal decanter and trays from Ikea. It was all about finding pieces that were well-designed, multifunctional, and comfortable to live with. This was the way I wanted to live, and it seemed that this style resonated with many of the readers of my books and of the magazine articles that featured the house. It was a way of respecting the old and bringing in the new with a personal point of view, a paring down to make the house relevant for today. I am passionate about saving old houses, and this is where it all started.

The newly discovered and restored fireplace became the focal point of the living room—and the house—with the mantel integrated into a paneled wall. A reproduction wing chair looks at home next to the fireplace, as it might have been in the early 1800s when the house was built.

Original beams found throughout the first floor are a reminder of the 1840s period of the house; wide-plank wood floors were installed to complement them. Because the house is located on Main Street, interior shutters are a perfect solution: the bottom ones can be adjusted for privacy, and keeping the panels above open lets in light. Bookshelves were installed in a shallow, unused space between the door and window.

After ripping out all the dark-wood cabinets that had been installed in the 1960s, I left the space open and added simple shelves for china and glasses. Keeping the refrigerator and freezer under the counter, with the dishwasher and range, reinforced the open plan of the kitchen. An old aquarium stand a friend was throwing away became an ideal island for storage and serving with a new granite top.

An 1820s mahogany sleigh bed found at a local estate sale is made up with simple white linen sheets and fits neatly in the small bedroom on the first floor. Uncovering the beams throughout reveals the structure of the house and sets the tone for honest natural materials, like the tree trunk found at a local garden center used as a bedside table. Seasonal branches and stones found on beach walks bring the outdoors in.

A SENSE OF PLACE

Old stone chimneys flank the 1820s white clapboard house, with Long Island privet hedges and an eighteenth-century wooden gate. Two dormers, which bring light to the guest bedrooms, were added in the 1930s.

One early fall morning about ten years ago, I went to see a house that was for sale on Main Street, down the road from mine. I had passed by it for years—an old-fashioned white cottage with green shutters and window boxes and a metal fence covered in wild sweet peas. But it was looking a bit sad and needed attention; wisteria blocked the path to the front door. I had always thought of it as "the sweet-pea house" and wondered who lived there.

Then one day, friends from the local historical society mentioned that the white house was for sale and, knowing that I had outgrown my well-loved but too-small place, suggested that I take a look.

Early the next morning I drove over and walked down the long path in back of the house, and to my surprise it led all the way to the river. Through a maze of brambles, I saw a cracked concrete pool, a sagging wooden outhouse, a derelict garage, and a chicken coop with little doors at the bottom. It was misty by the water, and there was a planked boardwalk to the dock and crumbling boathouse. I still remember how quiet it was; I could hear the leaves falling to the ground. Two perfect white swans swam to the dock as I was looking out, and that was it. I had to live here.

It turned out that there would be a tag sale that weekend, so I stayed and went through the house. I wanted a guest room or two: it had four. I was hoping

The paneled door and sidelights with paneling below are original to the house, but the posts with decorative brackets were added later. The slamming sound of the screen door in summer adds to the old-fashioned ambience.

for a fireplace: there were five. The kitchen was big enough for my white farm table, and I spied remnants of a chimney that rose from a cooking stove from years ago.

Initials had been etched into the front sitting-room window, so of course I wondered whose they were. I was told that the house was built in 1728, but my instinct—and research—made it more like 1810 to 1820; the residence had been thoroughly renovated in the 1930s.

The windows and raised wood paneling in the front part of the house were early and intact, and I discovered that the town's doctor had owned the house in the 1870s, which was when the back section with the kitchen had been added. I found big wooden cupboards and a small back porch, as well as a claw-foot tub and pedestal sink in the house's single bathroom that had both seen better days. But none of that made any difference. All I could really see were the rooms in shades of white, the linoleum stripped from the floors, and the windows washed.

By spring, after months of negotiation, it was all sorted out. With the purchase of the house came half of the narrow, wooded island across from the dock, a moldy old rowboat, bushel baskets for picking apples from the trees, closets filled with moths, piles of used books—and lots of potential. Closing

Over a tiny fireplace in the sitting room, a contemporary photograph of books and a row of white bowls bring a sense of modernity to the setting.

The sitting room has sheer white linen curtains at the windows, white canvas slipcovers on the sofa and wing chair, and a natural sisal rug to keep it light and airy. Because of the room's beautiful morning light, I often find house guests here early in the day, reading quietly.

Above: There is nothing better than the smell of fresh laundry from the clothesline or pillows and bed linens that have been aired on an early spring day.
Opposite: An extra pair of chairs can be pulled out when needed at the table.

day was sunny and warm, the lake path filled with the scent of lilacs and mock orange. I could now see all the daffodils in the field and apple trees in bloom. I was home. And I always loved a challenge.

I bought the house "as is," and of course my father, brothers, architect, and contractor friends had all come to see my new obsession before the closing. I received many warnings about how much time and money it would take for me to turn this around, but I didn't want to hear it. My nieces and nephews began to visit and take the canoe out to paddle around the island, fish off the dock, and throw stones at the beehives. It was an adventure for them, and for me.

Yet, as we explored the property, nine twenty-yard dumpsters were being filled with debris, and construction trucks littered the front lawn. I took down the chain-link fence and removed the concrete pool (with various science projects growing in it). I couldn't figure out why there was a pool in the front yard by the road. I still can't.

The first night I stayed in the house, I was awakened by birds flying through the ceiling into my bedroom. The water was rusty, the windows kept breaking, and the stairs to the basement were just two-by-fours nailed together. When I climbed down them early one morning to turn on the hot-water heater so I could take a bath, the stairs collapsed beneath me.

One wall of the living room has a grid of storage boxes, creating a wall-to-wall and floor-to-ceiling bookcase. Books are loosely organized in sections: art and photography, design and architecture, gardening and cooking.

My circa-1820s bed seems to fit just right in this old house. A pair of vintage nickel sconces has been refitted as reading lamps. The rugged pine-plank floors are painted with white deck paint, which makes the small space seem bigger.

Not every room in the house is white: the guest room is a soft, warm gray, and the twin beds are made up with crisp gray-and-white striped sheets. A vintage wicker table between the beds holds a lamp, clock, water carafe, candles, and magazines to make friends feel at home.

After crawling up to the first-floor kitchen, I called the painter (my friend Ralf, who was also a fire-department volunteer), who was supposed to work that morning. He took one look at my poor leg, called 911, and after a day in the ER I found that I had to stay off it for weeks. So I was quarantined upstairs in my unfinished bedroom in an unfinished house and couldn't do more than shuffle to the makeshift bathroom with my cast on.

The crew would arrive about 7:00 a.m. every day and start working by 7:15. Pete, the contractor, would write down everyone's order for coffee on a piece of scrap wood to take to the deli; he always added a cup of tea for me in his thick carpenter's pencil. Each morning he'd stop in and we'd go over the work that needed to be done. Everything was rotten. The beams needed reinforcing. When we turned on the watering system, the rusted pipes burst. The tub was about to fall through into the dining room. A bomb shelter behind a door in the basement was stocked with nothing but mold—and a case of old Cognac, which I shared with my friend Jim, the electrician.

But we carried on, changing course when needed. Six months later we were photographing the house for a feature in *Country Home* magazine about the renovation and my tips to surviving buying an old house. We continued with a series of articles over the next few years about how the chicken coop

An old twin bed painted white is set up as a daybed and tucks into one end of the boathouse. A perfect place to read and nap, it can also be an extra guest room in summer.

GUEST ROOM CHECKLIST

With a big family and city friends who enjoy a country getaway, I find that my guest rooms are always full. I like to have things ready and keep it simple for them and for me. Letting guests know what is fresh in the kitchen makes them feel at home. I like to keep the coffee/tea station ready for early risers, and a few bottles of wine and sparkling water in the refrigerator are always welcome. And Netflix streaming in the sitting/screening room is a plus.

BASICS FOR THE BEDROOM
Extra blanket for bed
Extra pillows
Comfortable chair for reading
Cozy throw for the chair
Good reading lamp
Water carafe and glass
Stack of assorted books and magazines
iPhone dock with music
Set of smartphone and laptop chargers
Wi-Fi and password for guests, if needed
Terry-cloth bathrobe
Scented candle with a light, neutral fragrance
Seasonal flowers, which can be as simple as one
    blossom in a glass or a jug of wildflowers
Hooks behind the door
Extra hangers for clothes
Full-length mirror
Luggage rack or bench for suitcases
Desk/table and chair for writing or using laptop
Notecards, notepaper, postcards, and stamps
Pens and pencils

BASICS FOR THE BATHROOM
Stack of towels and washcloths
Fresh guest soaps for the sink and shower/tub
Plenty of hooks for towels and robes
Box of tissues
Water glass

MEDICINE CABINET BASICS
Extra toothbrushes, toothpaste, mouthwash
Shampoo and conditioner
Moisturizing lotion
Bath salts and shower gel
Disposable razors
Cotton swabs and cotton balls
Nail polish remover

FIRST-AID KIT BASICS
Adhesive bandages
Antiseptic
Rubbing alcohol
Thermometer
Tweezers
Cough drops
Aspirin and/or pain-relief tablets

The guest bathroom's old claw-foot tub was salvaged and given new life with fresh nickel fittings.
The dreary linoleum floor was replaced with gray slate tiles for an updated look.

became a guest cottage, how the machine shop/garage was transformed into a summer studio, and how the decrepit boathouse evolved into an idyllic place for weekend dinners and drinks with friends, swans still stopping by.

My favorite accessory became a wagon from Home Depot that I painted black and used first to haul debris and then wine and glasses, plates and napkins down to the boathouse. We've had a family wedding-rehearsal dinner here, a bridal shower, book-club meetings, an art opening, my parents' wedding anniversary party, historical society sessions, pop-up shop events, and Christmas Eve celebrations every year. Magazine editors and catalog stylists continue to use the property as a backdrop for stories and promotions, and now photos of my house and gardens appear on Pinterest, Tumblr, and Instagram.

This house has become the home I envisioned that first morning I walked down to the lake. My house was here when the Civil War was brewing, when Walt Whitman wrote *Leaves of Grass* and Emily Dickinson her poems. My house was here when the women in town planted lilacs along Main Street in memory of Lincoln's assassination, when nineteenth-century author and editor Mary Louise Booth lived down the street, and when the suffragists were marching. I like to think I've brought the house back to life while keeping its history and architectural integrity intact. Now, it's my turn to be the steward of this house, this place, at this time.

The back of the property is wooded and has a path, bordered by ferns and rhododendrons, that leads to the dock and boathouse.

On this old farmhouse property, there are several outbuildings—a tiny outhouse, a light-filled studio (above), and an old chicken coop (opposite)—but my favorite is the boathouse at the end of the walk down to the river.

HOME/WORK

Working with the fireplace burning and a pot of tea steaming in fall, or walking to the boathouse with laptop and iPhone in spring—this new office style suits me. Email, conference calls, and overnight shipping make it so much easier to manage projects from home. And "reply all" is the new office meeting.

My home makes it simple to keep me inspired and stay self-motivated. There's always a lot to do, but I have all the space I need here. When I walk to the mailbox at the end of the driveway and put the red flag up for the day's outgoing mail, magazines from around the world are waiting: *Donna Hay Magazine* from Australia, *The World of Interiors* from London, and *The New Yorker*. I still get the *New York Times* delivered; the thud of the paper against the white wooden gate is a reassuring morning sound. And, though I sometimes work at the kitchen table or down at the boathouse, I usually head downstairs to my office—not a long commute. Here I have two long folding tables covered with linen drop cloths and upholstered benches along the sides; scanners, monitors, laptops, and hard drives are lined up at one end. Freelance assistants work with me, depending on the nature of the project, and it's good to have a dedicated workspace that I can leave behind when I want to.

No matter how much time I spend online, on Pinterest, and elsewhere, tear sheets and clippings are stacked precariously at my end of the table. I still enjoy pinning images and lists to old-fashioned bulletin boards. Rolling Metro shelving keeps magazines and design books at hand and covered bins are filled with fabric swatches, flooring samples, and paint decks for design projects I'm working on.

I've figured out a simple lunch plan for visiting clients and colleagues: it's

TADAO ANDO — LIGHT AND WATER

A MAGAZINE CURATED BY MAISON MARTIN MARGIELA — A MAGAZINE #1

VIVRE & TRAVAILLER

N ZOOB +M−7

PIET BOON

IN|EX WOLTERINCK — TERRA

Wolterinck

DESIGN IN BLACK & WHITE — Janelle McCulloch

COULEUR & HABITAT

CHAMBRES A COUCHER

PRICIA
LLS

contemporary natural — phyllis richardson / solvi dos santos

THE PRINCES OF IRELAND — Edward Rutherfurd

THE WITTGENSTEIN HOUSE

The Hotel Book

or Living — Bedrock

THE HOUSES OF IRELAND

Seaside Interiors

RY — VIKING

A SENSE OF THE COUNTRY — GARDEN TOOLS

ITALIAN COUNTRY — SABINO

Voyages en Italie

BELDEGREEN — THE BED

M and Decoration

PURE STYLE OUTSIDE — JANE CUMBERBATCH

MARY EMMERLING'S ROMANTIC COUNTRY

SET with STYLE

COLIN COWIE WEDDINGS

Hugh Newell Jacobsen, Architect

POTTERYBARN HOME

David Chipperfield — Architectural Works 1990–2002

DRIVING TOURS — ITALY

SEASHORE STYLE — ANDREA SPENCER

TH A HOUSE

A Secret Quest

Design

THE BOOK OF TEA

Living in the Countryside

Modern Architecture since 1900 — Curtis

In the company of stone

THE WAY WE LIVE

The office was carved out of the original dark and dank cellar. Wainscoting painted warm gray covers the rough walls; a large jute rug warms up the space; and two long folding tables covered in linen drop cloths transform the space. The fireplace surround was built on an existing chimney wall with old stones from the house's exterior.

a nice change to sit by the fire or have lunch on the porch in nice weather—especially for those who come out from the city for the day. A fresh salad with grilled bread or roasted pumpkin soup on cool days is easy to whip up and not too disruptive.

Volunteering with local historical societies is now a big part of my work life and my new passion: restoring old houses, creating museum exhibitions, researching the history and accomplishments of people from the past. My stash of architecture books is in great demand, whether to help identify a pilaster on a mid-nineteenth-century fireplace or to see how exterior door trim was applied in 1820. In these books, I can spend hours time-traveling through the houses, mostly from New England, with their lasting symmetry and craftsmanship.

The studio at the back of the property is the perfect place to do photo shoots, and even though I have been streamlining my possessions—my "props"—for some time now, I still have closets and cupboards filled with linens, glassware, and china when I need them.

The ability to provide visuals for websites and blogs is a click away for me, but the need for content is insatiable. So my home's natural setting is filled with inspiration for all the work I do. Following the seasons and how they translate to home design influence my work in a significant way, whether it is choosing a color palette or lighting fixture or determining how to approach an outdoor living space. Indoors and out, my home is the backdrop for my life and work.

Rows of Metro shelving keep stacks of books and magazines in order and can be moved around if necessary to reconfigure the room for presentations. The old and new beams have been painted white to make them consistent, and to reflect more light.

HOME/WORK CHECKLIST

*Although I now conduct most of my business online,
there is still a lot of paper lurking everywhere: tear sheets,
contracts, correspondence that I print out for reference
and safekeeping. And I find that I need bins, boxes, and
baskets for storage of paper, fabrics, material samples, and
magazines—not to mention shelving for my book addiction.
Using storage tools and office supplies that have a similar
palette helps to create a system out of chaos. Here is
a list of my favorite storage products and office supplies.*

STORAGE AND ORGANIZATION
Bigso boxes
Metro shelving
Lee Products expandable collator/organizer
Linen portfolios
Black binders
Muji linen bins in all sizes
Muji binders and clipboards
White binders with cover-image sleeve
Gaylord archival boxes
Uline cardboard boxes
My Passport Essential black hard drives
Clear plastic document folders

OFFICE SUPPLIES
MUJI
Clear pushpins
Stapler
White dustbins for recycling and paper
White cleaning system (dust mop)

STAPLES
Black uni-ball Rollerball pens with micro point

HOME DEPOT
Linen drop cloths for folding tables

An old garage used as a machine shop,
at the back of the property, was transformed
into a light-filled studio with a new sliding
barn door, an expansive window at one end,
and a standing-seam metal roof.

The old aquarium stand, used as a kitchen island in my former house, became a console table in the studio. It is now used for displays for work and meetings or as a bar or buffet for parties.

50 SHADES OF WHITE

White is basic and reassuring to me: it's always right; it always works. I appreciate the simplicity of white, the cleanliness and the purity of it, its blank slate. White represents serenity and calm in a busy life.

I find myself drawn to white houses, whether Shaker style, International Style, or Greek Revival. White picket fences and whitewashed gates, shutters, and railings all seem the way they should be. There is always texture, pattern, and natural color in shingles, brick paths, and plantings that work with them and around them.

The interiors I have created are in many shades of white, influenced I'm sure by the paint names I respond to: "Apron Strings," "Tuxedo Shirt," "Ironstone." I love looking at the names on paint charts; choosing various whites for ceiling, wall, and trim; envisioning them all together and as they transition from room to room, different shades with different moods. In the kitchen, I want a clean white; in the dining room, a soft-white backdrop for my china; in the living room, a warm, old-fashioned white for the bookshelves; in my bedroom, a calming white. A coat of white paint makes everything new again.

The old, wooden kitchen table I found in a barn is painted annually with shiny white enamel so newspaper smudges, spilled tea, or red wine can be cleaned up easily. White-painted cupboards hold stacks of white and cream china, the color palette creating a sense of order. White canvas slipcovers are my signature, and seasonal washings keep them fresh. Although some people

A new version of the classic Windsor chair looks right at home in this old house.
I usually bring in herbs from the garden at the first freeze and keep them in the windows
for light; I love snipping fresh herbs throughout the winter for cooking and fragrance.

may think white surfaces are difficult to keep clean, everything can be wiped with a sponge (white, of course) or thrown in the washer with a bit of bleach. It all seems low maintenance to me.

Changes of season mean different layers of white. Stacks of bed linens fill the shelves, from soft cream flannel for winter to crisp, cool linen for summer. Towels are cotton piqué during the summer, thick terry cloth in colder weather. Woolly knit throws work for fall, lighter cotton ones for spring. And I look forward to taking down the storm doors and windows each spring to replace them with white-painted screens. The garden has its own palette of whites, such as early spring snowdrops, peonies, and lilacs in May, and flowering privet hedges in June. In the winter, I plant paperwhite and amaryllis bulbs and bring a bit of the garden indoors, then later force hyacinths in glass jars on the window sills for fragrance and color—and as reminders of spring.

Of course, not everything is white: baskets are loaded with firewood and branches, piles of books and magazines fill every room, cutting boards and trays are stacked on shelves, sea sponges sit at sinks for washing up. Color and texture are everywhere, but the white setting keeps it all together and creates a look, an order, a personal, easy style. The "timelessness" of white in the house and its furnishings, in the things I collect and choose to live with—stones from the beach, eighteenth-century antiques, and today's industrial designs—all work together.

A few last roses at the end of their season are a nice touch in a guest-room window.
A water glass will do as a simple receptacle, and it fits nicely on the sill.

A still life with favorite things includes a large shell filled with stones from beach walks, a peony in full bloom, a stack of Chinese teacups tied with raffia, a pile of books, and creamware bowls and platters.

50 SHADES OF WHITE CHECKLIST

Over the years, I have found that I rely on certain basics for the home in all shades of white, especially paints and fabrics for simple makeovers. A coat of the right white paint can transform a room, a fence, a table, or a chair. And white slipcovers are a signature detail for me: they create a sense of calm, comfort, and cleanliness that I want in my home.

FABRICS

ROGERS & GOFFIGON
"Skye" in Whitewash
"Skye" in Croft
"Ruff" in Cloud

RALPH LAUREN HOME
"Snowfields Canvas" in Fog
"Addison Denim" in
    Bleached White
"Bar Harbour Cloth" in
    Sail White
"Faye Vintage Linen" in Lily
"Sunbaked Linen" in Canvas
"Farthingale" in Cream
"Collection Chino" in White
"Oak Bluff Matelasse" in
    White Seersucker

ROSE BRAND
Fine cotton gauze, available in
    broad seamless widths

OUTDOOR FABRICS

RALPH LAUREN HOME
"Coastal Plain" in Sailcloth

PERENNIALS
"Sail Cloth" in Sand
"Sunscreen" in Blanca

BED LINENS

EILEEN FISHER
Washed linen sheets in
    Pure White

ROUGH LINEN
Belgian linen sheeting in
    Strong White

PAINT

RALPH LAUREN
Chalk White
Picket Fence White
Journal White
Starch
Plaster White
Polo Mallet White

FARROW & BALL
Clunch
Cornforth White
Wimborne White
Ammonite

BENJAMIN MOORE
Simply White
Snow White
Decorators White

TABLEWARE

WEDGWOOD
"Wedgwood White"
"Jasper Conran White Bone"

ROYAL DOULTON
"1815"

CALVIN KLEIN
"Quay Porcelain"

SIMON PEARCE
"Brookfield" serveware

KAJ FRANCK FOR IITTALA
"Teema" in White

HEATH CERAMICS
"Chez Panisse" in Jicama

HARTLEY GREENS & CO
"Hunslet" mugs

DESIGN WITHIN REACH
Eva Zeisel "Granite" dishes

MUD AUSTRALIA
Assorted bowls in Milk

ASTIER DE VILLATTE
"Simple" plates

FURNITURE

DESIGN WITHIN REACH
Arne Jacobsen "Egg" chair
Eero Saarinen round
    "Pedestal" table
"Salt" Windsor chair

WEATHEREND ESTATE
FURNITURE
Oval settee

JOHN DERIAN COMPANY
"Field Bench with Back"
"Cove" sofa

GEORGE SMITH
Buttoned ottoman

LIGHTING

Isamu Noguchi paper shades
Anglepoise lamps
Bestlite lamps
Tizio lamps by Artemide

An oversize canvas bag is ready for shopping at the farmers market or flea market, keeping laundry separated, organizing samples in the office, or keeping things neatly stored in the car.

A PLACE FOR EVERYTHING

I love to arrange things. Filling the pantry, sorting the laundry, and stocking the linen cupboard create visual continuity and order that make mundane rituals more enjoyable and housekeeping more manageable. One can tell what's needed at a glance, see what works together, and assess the gaps that should be filled.

In his workshop, my father used to keep all his nails and screws in labeled jars and tools lined up by size, ready for action. Baby-food jars and coffee cans were his containers of choice, and probably of necessity in those early days of recycling, when we used what was available for another turn. Today, I save clear Mason jars with wired lids and takeout containers without advertising. Then I indulge myself buying pristine white enamel containers from Muji to supplement them. I also have a drawer filled with bits and balls of string—linen, cotton, jute, hemp—that I use for everyday tasks: wrapping packages, keeping recycled papers together, tying up plants. But I suspect I use string in part to justify keeping a string drawer, which gives me pleasure when I open it and see all the natural colors and textures in rows—a perfect, patterned design. Newspapers are stacked in a burlap storage bin for use as fire starters; when I go for a walk, I invariably come back with an armful of twigs I've picked up along the way for kindling. I fill baskets with bouquets of them to keep next to the fireplace, as well as smaller baskets of pinecones.

My books are not organized by color, as is trendy today, or by the Dewey Decimal System, as my librarian friends' bookshelves are. Instead, they're sorted into four general categories—gardening, architecture, photography, and design—and cookbooks fill a dedicated kitchen cabinet. Novels come and go

from the shelves, especially in this era of the iPad, but I use my design books and stacks of home-design magazines in my daily work, so keeping them in some kind of order is important. I'm still a tear-sheet as well as a Pinterest person, and the shelves in my office hold years of magazines and portfolios filled with magazine pages that have emotional significance or are references for a future design project.

My pantry is stocked with basics for the simple way I cook, and if I don't like the packaging, I repackage. Enlisting a label maker with favorite fonts, I decant liquids into old wine bottles and transfer flours and sugars into glass canisters. Shelves are filled with pastas and sauces, sundried tomatoes and sea salt, olive oils and vinegars. I don't need a lot of things; I just want what I have found to be tried and true. If I like something, I commit to it. I am the same way about clothes, china, and most everything else in my home. A friend once said that I was always consistent, and I took that as a compliment.

Much of what I have is behind closed doors, as the calm this creates is important to me, but collections and everyday tools for living are visually comforting when they are displayed in a deliberate way. Lining things up, making the most of small spaces, and putting tools of everyday life in order are, to me, an art form.

A Shaker peg rack—an easy storage solution for small spaces in every room, especially in narrow hallways and tight spaces—holds string market bags and aprons.

If they are well-designed objects, glass jugs and bottles can be arranged on a tray as a still life until they are ready to be used—as containers for flowers and herbs or for waters and juices at mealtime.

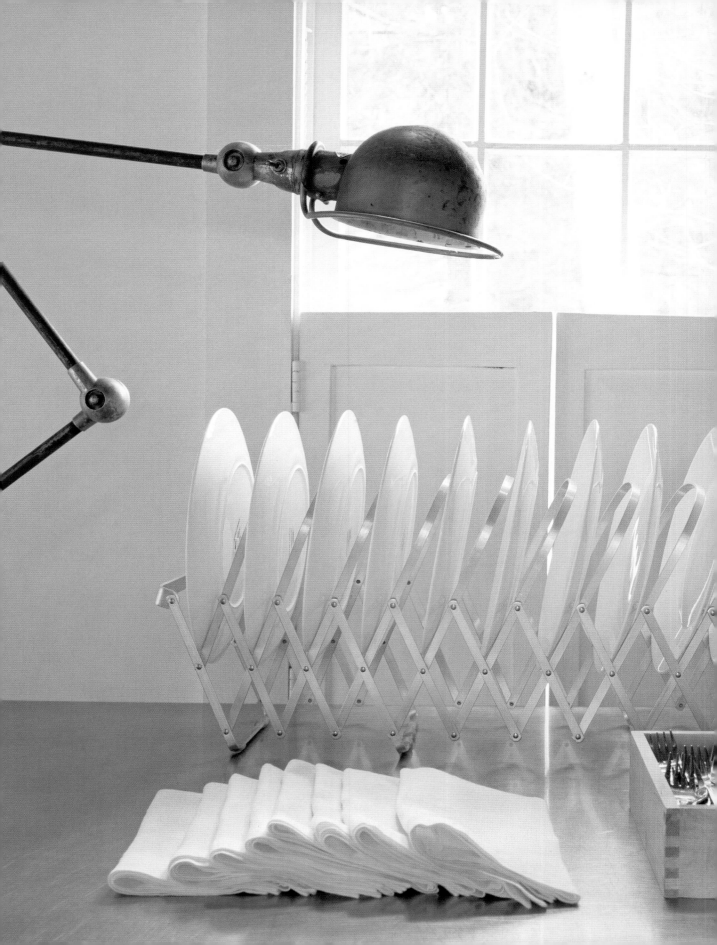

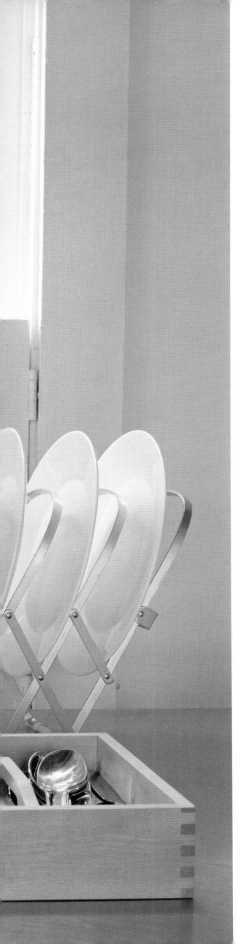

An aluminum folding organizer, called a collator, usually brings order to my tear sheets or project files, but is put to work here as a dessert-plate holder. Having folded napkins, forks, and spoons ready for the last course enables me to spend time enjoying my friends instead of rushing around. Arranging things on the serving table in advance and playing with the tabletop elements are part of the process I enjoy the most. I like to be able to use what I have and rethink the many ways to utilize household objects.

The ten kitchen tools I can't live without: jute string, white sponges, flour-sack towels, white knitted potholders, wine-bottle opener, Joyce Chen scissors, microplane grater, wooden tongs, black Muji spatula, and cast-iron pans.

Packaging and label typefaces affect my purchasing decisions—as evidenced in the arrangement of products seen in a glass-door cabinet. If the packaging isn't up to par, glass jars and white ceramic cups are great organizers and make everyday objects look better.

Although there is a proper laundry room downstairs, it's sometimes nice to iron linens in the daylight in the kitchen. A thick pad under the ironing board cover and scented waters for the steam iron make it an enjoyable experience.

Opposite: Behind the doors of a cupboard is a lifelong collection of glassware, from simple machine-made juice glasses to vintage pressed-glass tumblers and Swedish hand-blown goblets. Friends love to look inside and choose a favorite glass.

A PLACE FOR EVERYTHING CHECKLIST

Well-designed storage containers and bins make organizing things in drawers and cabinets a pleasure. A simple approach—keeping "like things" together and using color-coded boxes and bags—creates a unified look, which is always my goal. Whether in the food pantry, office supplies drawer, linen closet, or china cupboard, keeping things in jars, jugs, basket trays, or boxes makes finding what you need so much easier. Of course, companies specialize in systems for storage, but you can create your own using personal collections: everything from Mason jars and French jelly jars to odd pieces of pottery are put to use here.

KITCHEN/DINING ROOM TIPS

PANTRY
Use clear glass jars that enable you to see what's available at a glance.
Organize baking needs, spices, and condiments in separate sections.
Group provisions for specific meals together: pastas, olive oils, olives, sauces.

REFRIGERATOR + FREEZER
Group jams, jellies, and honey together.
Wrap and date dairy products such as butter and cheese.
Group juices, wines, waters, and sodas together.
Use clear bags when freezing food to be able to see the contents.
Label each freezer bag with date of storage to ensure freshness.

KITCHEN DRAWERS
Keep things neat and at the ready with dividers in bamboo, light wood, or wicker, using adjustable ones for utensils that are odd sizes.
Use kraft paper to line drawers.
Store small things in gift boxes without lids to keep them together.

CHINA CUPBOARD
Protect plates in stacks by placing in between the plates felt rounds or squares from a craft shop.
Use trays to keep teacups and coffee mugs on the shelf yet easy to access.
Keep platters, serving bowls, and dessert sets on plate racks, whether placed inside or outside of cupboards.

BEDROOM/BATH TIPS

LINEN CLOSET
Organize sheets by size of bed, then keep sets together tied with ribbon or, alternatively, put each set in one of its pillowcases.
Label shelves with contents so that they are easy to maintain.

MEDICINE CABINET
Use glass jars and bottles to hold cotton swabs and cotton balls.

I had always wanted a clean, well-lit laundry with room for sorting baskets, a counter to fold towels, and an ironing board at the ready. I like to keep things low and under the counter, with lots of storage, so after analyzing the basement and creating a big room for my office, I was able to carve out a space for the laundry, which does double duty as a flower arranging/planting room.

GOSHAWK

XVIII

STILL LIFES

Where others might feel that filling the top of a mantelpiece or coffee table is daunting, I love the opportunity to create something beautiful with my favorite things. Sometimes it is just one perfect object, sometimes a collection that has grown over time, sometimes a mix of containers and seasonal flowers. I enjoy showing friends' artwork, whether drawings, paintings, or photographs, and if I don't have wall space, I find a ledge or mantel to lean or stack them on. I love the juxtaposition of functional things like a large roll of string against an antique glass bell jar. Or putting all vases, glasses, decanters, and bowls together to create a mass of shapes or color. I tend to collect a lot of china and glass, which is put to work all the time, and when I need to, I raid the living room mantel for a big glass bowl or a hurricane lamp with a candle to put on the table for a dinner party. Things are always moving around here, and something as simple as a few pairs of straw slippers in a row, a swan feather, or a pile of stones picked up from the beach becomes interesting in a new way when it is added to a mix of tonal objects, used out of scale, or in an irreverent way. It's all very personal, and to me, that's what a home should be.

A corner of the fireplace mantel in the living room has a mix of accessories: Japanese black lacquer bowls, a glass vase, and a black glazed candlestick with a tall white candle.

Oversize white platters look good
on a wall and are at the ready if
needed for serving. Here, just one
is placed above the wainscoting, but
they can be displayed in groups as
well. Following spread: Bell jars, or
cloches in gardener's language,
come in many sizes and do much
more than protect seedlings.
A collection in various sizes, new
ones and old, is just as beautiful to
look at inside as when they are
being used in the garden.

Keeping glass containers together makes it easier to find a carafe, decanter, or vase when looking for the right shape for wine or an arrangement of flowers.

Different sizes of hurricane shades and candle holders massed on the fireplace mantel don't look cluttered because they are all either clear or white.

Sometimes flowers freshly picked from the garden look just as nice in a rustic basket used for gathering them before they are arranged. I have a collection of baskets that I use for harvesting flowers and herbs; for holding garden tools, firewood, and laundry; and for all kinds of chores around the house.

In the tradition of Japanese *wabi-sabi*, a single antique shoe form in wood with a fine patina (opposite) is singled out and displayed as a sculptural object. Old conch shells are pressed into service as doorstops.

AT TABLE

I grew up as the eldest of seven children, and meals at our family house were always casual, always big, always inclusive. If friends came over to do homework, they probably stayed for supper—it was no trouble to pull up another chair or set another plate on the table. My mother had the kettle on all the time, and tea was an important part of our lives. To celebrate a report card, a birthday, or other good news, a pot was made. If someone fell out of a tree or off a go-cart or had a bad day at school, a cup of tea was handed out with Band-Aids. It's still that way at my house, too.

When friends, family, and neighbors stop by, the kettle is always ready. Entertaining is not a big deal to me, as I have enough white plates to serve a hundred: a tableful of friends is my idea of a good time. I enjoy setting the table, celebrating spring, fall, or a holiday with flowering branches, bulbs, or, off season, a bunch of tulips from the grocery store in a jug.

In nice weather, it's drinks at the boathouse: everyone who has been here knows where to find us. When it's cool, you'll see hors d'oeuvres or antipasto on the kitchen table. A fire's going, and everyone gathers until we are ready to move to the dining room. When guests ask if they can help, I say yes. With someone stoking the fire, someone else opening wine, and another passing glasses, those who haven't met are now part of the family.

The dining room in this 1820s house has no electricity, and there I have an old wood-and-wire chandelier; when I give someone the job of lighting the candles, dinner becomes an occasion. The menus are simple as I want to be at the table, not worrying about the next course or what's happening in the oven. Pastas, homemade pizzas, quesadillas, frittatas, and lots of fresh vegetables and salads are the usual fare. My dishes are easy to prepare in advance, easy to stretch if unexpected guests arrive, and easy to save for leftovers.

Because many people have food preferences or restrictions, I try to make meals modular so that there is something for all my guests. A shop down the road has freshly roasted chickens; if someone is avoiding carbs or cheese or has allergies, I pick one up, customize it with rosemary and lemons, and add it to the mix. Big pitchers of iced water with sprigs of mint from the garden sit on the table, usually accompanied by wine and beer.

Soft, generous napkins are more practical for me than stiff, starched ones. And serving family style or buffet style allows people to choose how much or how little they would like. Summer meals revolve around what's at the farm stand, which means tomatoes and corn are often part of the theme. And for dessert, the season calls for bowls of blackberries with whipped cream or a lemon tart.

In colder weather, roasted vegetables, pastas with herbs, and grilled breads with olive oil are my go-to meals. A tarte Tatin with apples or pears not only smells wonderful in the oven but is an easy and festive way to end an autumn supper. We may sit around the dining table for hours or move to the living room for dessert in front of the fire. It's all about being comfortable and making everyone feel at home.

A runner of raw canvas instead of a traditional tablecloth sets the tone for a light lunch. Bell jars keep cheeses fresh and add height to a buffet tablescape—a stylist's trick that is both sensible and stylish.

SPRING STUDIO LUNCH

A drizzly spring weekend was the excuse for a luncheon in the studio. The big table was positioned by the window with a view of the budding trees, and small zinc pots scattered on the table were filled with different blossoms. Flowering quince branches, always a favorite of mine, were harvested from a shrub that came with the house. Recycled clear wine bottles were filled with water and wine at either end of the table.

The long, stainless-steel worktable takes on a new life as a bar and buffet server, set with drinks, cheeses, and a tray for tea and coffee later.

SUMMER OUTDOOR DINING

The boathouse is a magical place for drinks or a dinner party . . . just walking down to the water makes it an occasion. There is always an evolving backdrop of trees and plants that changes with the seasons.

Sturdy linens and straw place mats seem just right for a boathouse luncheon for friends. A simple lunch would be a pasta salad filled with vegetables, crusty bread, and peaches for dessert with mint water and a light wine—easy to transport by wagon down to the water. A peaceful setting, rain or shine.

White cheeses with a drizzle of honey and lemon verbena jelly make a cheese board summery. Opposite: An easy way to transform a pint container of ice cream or gelato into something special is to turn it upside down on a platter and surround it with berries. I like using blackberries and blueberries together and serving it with a silver soup spoon.

Keeping it simple—with a one-plate meal, goblets for wine or water, and light
straw place mats—makes it easy to take a dinner party to an outside table.

FALL HARVEST LUNCH

Opposite: An arugula salad is one of my go-to recipes. One option is to add fennel slices to fresh arugula, as well as grated Parmesan and toasted pine nuts, then tossing with fresh lemon juice and olive oil. Other versions include grapefruit sections, sundried tomatoes, and black olives; or fresh chopped tomatoes and mint. Pages 164–65: A memorable farm-to-table supper was hosted by Isabella Rossellini at her nearby organic farm for the Bellport-Brookhaven Historical Society. I pulled out all my china and linens and glasses to set the table for one hundred in her field. Our chef friends created a meal with donations from local farms and vineyards.

SPICY PUMPKIN SOUP

I found a recipe for Southwestern Pumpkin Soup on Ronda Rice Carman's *Soup on Sunday* post, and it was the inspiration for my version with lots of spice for cold autumn weekends. It's a perfect simple starter in a small cup or bowl for lunch or dinner, and a large bowl is just right as a main course with salad and crunchy, rustic bread for a country lunch.

Serves 4 to 6

INGREDIENTS

    4 cups vegetable stock
    1 cup light cream
    30 ounces (3 ¾ cups) canned pumpkin purée
    1 teaspoon ground cumin
    ½ teaspoon chili powder
    ½ teaspoon ground coriander
    ½ teaspoon ground nutmeg
    Sea salt and freshly ground pepper to taste

GARNISHES

    Grated Parmesan (1 teaspoon per serving to sprinkle on top)
    Fresh cilantro, shredded (1 teaspoon per serving)
    Toasted pumpkin seeds or pine nuts (½ teaspoon per serving)
    Herb pan-fried croutons

DIRECTIONS

1. In a heavy medium-sized saucepan, bring the stock and cream to a boil. Whisk in the pumpkin, cumin, chili powder, coriander, and nutmeg.

2. Reduce the heat to medium, and simmer for about 15 minutes, or until the soup thickens slightly and the flavors blend.

3. Season with salt and pepper, and ladle into bowls.

4. Garnish with Parmesan, cilantro, pumpkin seeds or pine nuts, and croutons, and serve while hot.

ARUGULA-FENNEL SALAD

Baby arugula is a flavorsome fall or winter salad base. I dress it with a simple squeeze of lemon and a drizzle of olive oil, shavings of Parmesan, and a toss of pine nuts as a starter for a meal. Add grapefruit wedges, slices of fennel, mandarin oranges, sundried tomatoes and black olives, or ricotta salata when it is a more important part of the menu.

INGREDIENTS

    8 ounces (about 2 to 4 bunches) arugula
    10 to 12 shavings of Parmesan
    1 medium-sized fennel bulb, rough outer layer removed and root end trimmed, thinly sliced
    ¼ cup pan-roasted pine nuts
    1 medium fresh lemon
    1 to 2 tablespoons extra-virgin olive oil
    Sea salt and freshly ground black pepper to taste

DIRECTIONS

1. Toast the pine nuts in a small cast-iron skillet over a low heat until golden brown.

2. In a large serving bowl, toss the arugula with Parmesan, fennel, and pan-roasted pine nuts.

3. Squeeze the juice from the lemon over the greens.

4. Drizzle olive oil over the greens and toss thoroughly.

5. Season with salt and pepper when ready to serve.

WINTER WHITE DINNER

My friend and neighbor Marité is a food stylist and talented chef. One winter weekend we decided to host a white dinner party together, inviting a group of friends to my house for the evening. I set the table and the scene, and Marité prepared the food. She started with little black-pepper Parmesan shortbreads, which were hard to stop eating, then a salad of endive with pink grapefruit, fennel, and Parmesan slices, served with warm ricotta drizzled with oil and thyme—plus a stack of grilled rustic bread. Our main course was angel-hair pasta spun into a nest and topped with toasted breadcrumbs, garlic, and herbs. A fresh fig tart with vanilla-flavored whipped cream was the finale.

Grilled peasant bread served on a small wooden board becomes
another course when paired with warmed ricotta cheese, a good Italian
olive oil, and a sprinkle of sea salt and fresh thyme leaves.

BLACK-PEPPER PARMESAN SHORTBREAD

My friend Marité Acosta, a chef and food stylist, makes these for hors d'oeuvres at her house, and they've now become sought after at my dinner parties, too.

Yields about 30 shortbreads

INGREDIENTS

    2 cups all-purpose flour
    1 teaspoon fine sea salt
    16 tablespoons (2 sticks) unsalted butter, room temperature
    ¼ cup granulated sugar
    ¾ cup Parmesan, coarsely grated
    1 ½ teaspoons fresh thyme, finely chopped
    2 teaspoons lemon zest, finely grated
    2 teaspoons freshly ground black pepper

DIRECTIONS

Preheat oven to 325°F and line two 14 by 16-inch baking sheets with parchment paper.

1. Sift the flour and salt into a large bowl. Beat the butter and sugar together in a stand mixer on medium-high until fluffy, about 5 minutes. Add the Parmesan, thyme, lemon zest, and black pepper and continue mixing until incorporated. Add the flour to the mixture and beat until just combined.

2. Form into heaping teaspoon- or tablespoon-sized balls and chill on a baking sheet in the refrigerator for about one hour until firm. When ready to bake, space the shortbreads about one inch apart on the baking sheets and bake for 15 to 18 minutes, or until just golden brown on the bottoms. They should remain pale in color on top.

3. Move to a cooling rack until cooled and serve.

NOTES

These may also be made ahead and stored in the freezer. They take about 15 minutes to bake from frozen and smell delicious when baking.

If you're going to freeze these, first place the balls of dough on a plate or small baking sheet and put in the freezer. When dough is frozen, pop them into a baggie and keep in the freezer until ready to bake and serve.

TOASTED BREADCRUMB PASTA

The best olive oil possible and freshest garlic really make the difference in this simple dish.

Serves 4 to 6

INGREDIENTS

    1 pound dry angel-hair pasta
    2 cups panko (or other breadcrumbs)
    5 tablespoons extra-virgin olive oil, divided, plus more to finish
    4 to 5 cloves garlic, finely chopped
    Pinch of red pepper flakes
    Zest of 1 lemon, finely grated
    Grated Parmesan
    Sea salt (for pasta water and for seasoning)

DIRECTIONS

1. Bring a large pot of salted water to a boil over high heat and add the pasta. Cook until al dente according to package instructions. When straining, save and set aside about 2 cups of the cooking liquid.

2. In a medium bowl, combine the panko with 3 tablespoons of the olive oil. Using your fingers, mix in the olive oil to evenly coat the crumbs. Toast panko in a large sauté pan over medium-high heat until golden brown. Remove to the bowl to cool.

3. In the same pan, heat the remaining 2 tablespoons of olive oil over medium heat and stir in the garlic, cooking until softened and fragrant, about 4 minutes. Add the warm pasta to the pan along with about ½ cup of the reserved pasta water and toss well with the garlic and oil until most of the water is absorbed, adding more if needed for moisture.

4. Sprinkle half of the breadcrumbs over the pasta and a pinch of red pepper flakes and toss to combine.

5. To serve: In a large bowl, add the pasta and generously top with the remaining bread crumbs, lemon zest, grated Parmesan, and salt to taste. Drizzle olive oil over the top and serve.

HOME FOR THE HOLIDAYS

Christmas has always been an important time for our family—a time to gather and a time to enjoy certain rituals. The smell of a fresh evergreen tree and the wood smoke from the fireplace bring me right back to all the Christmases past—my mother baking, my looking for the perfect gift, all sitting down at the table together with Bing Crosby music playing in the background. Although some of the rituals change as the family evolves, some remain unchanged. I like to show all the home movies of our family holidays, much to the dismay of certain siblings, and pull out family photos and tell stories. I've taken on the role of family historian, and feel it's so important to keep these moments recorded. I'm glad my father documented the family with his movie camera all those years, but now, of course, the films are projected from my laptop and the old photos are scanned and viewed in slide-show mode.

I try to make an annual holiday card (even though I'm sending more and more by email these days), and every year Christmas Eve dinner is at my house. The red-and-white-checked linens are pulled out from the cupboard, and the Prosecco is chilled.

Living on Long Island near the water, it's easy to find inspiration in nature for holiday decorating. A fresh-cut fir tree—with simple white lights and a burlap-wrapped stand—is a natural look for an outdoor setting.

My old ice skates from seventh grade are a reminder of winters past: walking to the pond after school with a thermos of hot chocolate and layers of scarves and gloves to keep warm.

Sometimes the tree is laden with all the ornaments I have. Other times it's only decorated with a string of white lights. But the candles are lit, the firewood is stocked, and holiday music is playing—these are the givens. My brothers still wrap their gifts in newspaper and use Magic Markers, and my sister and I always wonder if we're giving each other the same thing. And I am always happy to receive new books that I can't wait to read by the fire, once everyone has gone, which is how it's been since I was very young.

I find that it's the simple things that are the most enduring. I love filling the house with big bouquets of branches, and start potting up paperwhites and amaryllis at Thanksgiving to bring greenery and white blossoms into the house. Bowls of tangerines remind me of my grandmother, who always put a tangerine and walnuts in each of our stockings—a tradition from her English childhood.

And, as it is the season for spending time with friends and family, there are many occasions for entertaining. From drinks parties for friends and tea by the fire to Christmas Eve dinner with the family, keeping it simple and enjoying the time together is what it's all about for me.

Taking time to sit by the fire with fir-scented candles and votives is the best way to get in the holiday spirit. Pots of paperwhites growing throughout the season are fragrant and decorative.

Bouquets of black berries from the privet hedge and rosehips from the rosebushes join sprays of greenery in baskets and buckets that are placed throughout the house. Plaid wool throws hanging from a peg rack in the entrance hall are ready for cool evenings, and a pine garland along the stair rail welcomes all with its fragrance.

A mix of fir, pine, juniper, cedar, and pinecones creates texture in wreaths and sprays. A cream-colored flannel stocking with vintage buttons and an ironstone bowl filled with white candy canes are old-fashioned touches in this old house.

A vintage ornament nestled in a found bird's nest (above) and a
stack of Shaker wood boxes tied with black ribbon and a sprig of boxwood
(opposite) are reminders of a natural Christmas and a simpler time.

MAY ALL YOUR
CHRISTMAS DREAMS
COME TRUE...

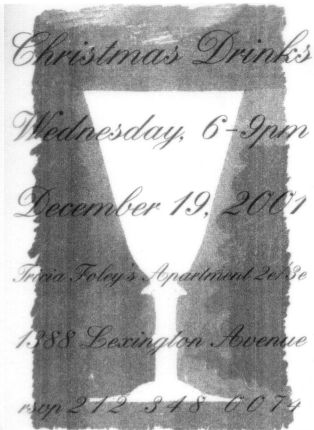

Christmas Drinks

Wednesday, 6–9pm

December 19, 2001

Tricia Foley's Apartment 2e/3e

1388 Lexington Avenue

rsvp 212 348 0074

Sherries & Savories

At Home
SUNDAY
DECEMBER 8, 2002
12 NOON - 3 PM

Tricia Foley's House

HAPPY CHRISTMAS

Each year, I look forward to making a card for the season. Whether the image is a sepia-toned photograph, a feather, an etching, or classical typography—the constant is a message from the heart.

wishing
you a
peaceful
holiday

I always harvest the last of the greenery and berries of the season to use for embellishing wreaths and decorating packages. I love to attach a bit of the garden and woods of my property to the presents I send to friends around the country.

Holly is a traditional, holiday green, and I use it with napkins tied with string and for packages wrapped in faux-bois and simple kraft papers.

Amaryllis, a white winter flower, is a favorite of mine, whether displayed in
single flower bouquets or potted in terra-cotta with moss. A slice of
mango wood is a serving board for hors d'oeuvres or a tray for drinks.

The sideboard is set up for a holiday party with a silver punch bowl used as a wine cooler. A white egg-shaped ornament, tied with a brown velvet ribbon, is hung on the candle sconce for an elegant holiday decoration.

HOME FOR THE HOLIDAYS CHECKLIST

I always make lists and put them on my calendar so I have a plan. The most important thing is to start with preparations early, so it is not overwhelming at the last minute. It is so easy to find bulbs and pot them in November and enjoy them growing throughout the house, to take time to create a holiday card one Sunday afternoon while watching old movies, and to stock up on drinks and provisions along the way. Having a set plan makes these annual rituals a pleasure, not a chore.

DECORATING

NOVEMBER 1:
Clean and plant terra-cotta pots.
Plant amaryllis bulbs (4–6 weeks to bloom).
Get fresh moss.

NOVEMBER 15:
Plant paperwhites (3–4 weeks to bloom).
Check candle stock and fill in.
Order firewood for delivery.

NOVEMBER 30:
Clear fall/Thanksgiving plants and pumpkins.
Plant more paperwhites.
Prepare fresh garlands for the outside door.
Buy ready-made wreaths and customize with
    berries and branches.

DECEMBER 1–10:
Get tree stands ready.
Check lights and replace bulbs when needed.
Put up tree and keep watered.
Decorate the tree.
Arrange branches and flowers.
Enlist little ones to help bake cookies.

ENTERTAINING

NOVEMBER 1–10:
Put dates on calendar for gatherings with
    friends and family.
Stock up on wine, cider, and Prosecco.
Buy nuts, crackers, and bottles of water along
    the way.

DECEMBER 1–10:
Wash glasses, iron linens, and polish silver.
Host Sunday tea/drinks party for friends.

DECEMBER 11–25:
Stock firewood and kindling at fireplaces.
Get large platters, bowls, and serving
    boards ready.
Set table and get buffet table staged.
Christmas Eve family gathering.

GIFT GIVING

NOVEMBER:
Work on holiday card.
Buy holiday stamps or design them.
Go to local holiday markets for finds.
Start ordering gifts online.
Set up gift-wrapping station.
Start wrapping . . . make sure to put
    tags on gifts!

DECEMBER 1–10:
Send out holiday cards.
Start putting gifts under tree.
Mail gifts to faraway friends and family.
Finish gift wrapping.
Put aside hostess gifts so they are ready to go:
    flavored salts, honey, jams, lemon vinegar.

DECEMBER 11–31:
Enjoy the season!

An easy winter-white dessert—a snowball-like scoop of vanilla ice cream is rolled in coconut flakes.
For a prepared-ahead treat, put in muffin tins in the freezer and serve when needed.

An overscale wreath from the local garden center becomes even more dramatic with the addition of boxwood branches tucked in to add texture and fullness.

ACKNOWLEDGMENTS

This book would not have happened without the encouragement of my good friend Doug Turshen—I thank him first, for his support and his elegant design, turning all my favorite home stories into a beautiful book. And many thanks to Sandy Gilbert Freidus and Philip Reeser, who both enabled me to realize my vision.

To all my photographer friends and colleagues, who have captured the spirit of my home and style in these pages, I give my heartfelt gratitude: Bill Abranowicz, Quentin Bacon, John Bessler, Anita Calero, Gemma Comas, Marili Forastieri, Jeff McNamara, Matthew Mead, Eric Piasecki, Laura Resen, Michael Skott, Bill Steele, and Simon Upton. To Jacqui Small for sharing photos of our table setting, and to André Junget, who illustrated my compound of little buildings and made sense of it all.

To Jeff Weinstein, my appreciation for helping me put into words the story of my house, and to David Huang for his patience with our image retrieval and for his "just right" layouts. And to Deborah Geltman for her reassuring advice as always, and Marité Acosta and Candy Argondizza, who bought my old house, became friends, and are always up for my schemes, making beautiful meals along the way.

To Isabella Rossellini, whose lovely words set the tone for the book, and the lifestyle we both love.

And, at Rizzoli, I extend my thanks to publisher Charles Miers; Elizabeth Smith, who fine-tuned the text; and Susan Lynch, who oversaw production.

PHOTO CREDITS

First published in the United States of America in 2015 by:

Rizzoli International Publications, Inc.
300 Park Avenue South
New York, NY 10010
www.rizzoliusa.com

Copyright © 2015 by Tricia Foley

Rizzoli Editors: Sandy Gilbert Freidus and Philip Reeser
Rizzoli Production Manager: Susan Lynch
Designers: Doug Turshen with David Huang

ISBN: 978-0-8478-4641-2
Library of Congress Control Number: 2015933004

Distributed to the U.S. trade by Random House, New York

Printed and bound in China

2015 2016 2017 2018 / 10 9 8 7 6 5 4 3 2 1

HAPPY FALL!
Marlo - Ted